Unwinding Anxiety

Mind|Spirit Connection

45-Day Workbook Journal

Other Books in This Series:

Unwinding Anxiety: Free Your Mind, Get Your Life Back

Unwinding Anxiety Body Connection: 45-Day Workbook Journal

For more information and to sign up for the 5-day Mindfulness Challenge, go to:

https://bit.ly/2OYOXoY

Inside, you will find:

- ***45 Days of Workbook and Journal Pages*** for you to track your experience and progress with these practices and methods for releasing and dismantling anxiety.

- Excerpts from ***Unwinding Anxiety: Free Your Mind, Get Your Life Back (see Appendix)***

    With instructions for:

    - Body scan
    - Release Your Tension
    - Calm-abiding Meditation
    - Contemplations
    - Compassion – Tonglen
    - Lovingkindness – Maitri

"The body is workable. The mind is workable… This is workable because no matter how bad it feels in the moment, or scary, it's a condition that you can break down inch by inch, breath by breath. **It takes practice. Trust in the process and keep working it. Keep noticing. Keep breathing."**

May you be well on your journey… make friends with your mind.

And now begins your Workbook and Journal Pages....enjoy the journey!

Date: _____

Before you practice, check in with yourself.

- ❖ MIND

    Quiet   Very Noisy

    1   2   3   4   5

- ❖ BODY

    Relaxed   Very Tense

    1   2   3   4   5

- ❖ SPIRIT

    At ease   Very Uneasy

    1   2   3   4   5

The practice(s) I am working with today: (check which one(s) you feel drawn to)

- ○ Body scan
- ○ Release Your Tension
- ○ Calm-abiding Meditation
- ○ Contemplations
- ○ Compassion – Tonglen
- ○ Lovingkindness - Maitri

How will I continue to care for myself today?_____
_____

My Journal for today… thoughts, notes, experiences…

Date: _____

Before you practice, check in with yourself.

- ❖ MIND

Quiet				Very Noisy
1	2	3	4	5

- ❖ BODY

Relaxed				Very Tense
1	2	3	4	5

- ❖ SPIRIT

At ease				Very Uneasy
1	2	3	4	5

The practice(s) I am working with today: (check which one(s) you feel drawn to)
- ○ Body scan
- ○ Release Your Tension
- ○ Calm-abiding Meditation
- ○ Contemplations
- ○ Compassion – Tonglen
- ○ Lovingkindness - Maitri

How will I continue to care for myself today?_____

_____

My Journal for today... thoughts, notes, experiences...

Date: _____

Before you practice, check in with yourself.

- ❖ MIND

Quiet				Very Noisy
1	2	3	4	5

- ❖ BODY

Relaxed				Very Tense
1	2	3	4	5

- ❖ SPIRIT

At ease				Very Uneasy
1	2	3	4	5

The practice(s) I am working with today: (check which one(s) you feel drawn to)

- ○ Body scan
- ○ Release Your Tension
- ○ Calm-abiding Meditation
- ○ Contemplations
- ○ Compassion – Tonglen
- ○ Lovingkindness - Maitri

How will I continue to care for myself today?_____

_____

My Journal for today… thoughts, notes, experiences…

Date: _____

Before you practice, check in with yourself.

- ❖ MIND

Quiet				Very Noisy
1	2	3	4	5

- ❖ BODY

Relaxed				Very Tense
1	2	3	4	5

- ❖ SPIRIT

At ease				Very Uneasy
1	2	3	4	5

The practice(s) I am working with today: (check which one(s) you feel drawn to)
- ○ Body scan
- ○ Release Your Tension
- ○ Calm-abiding Meditation
- ○ Contemplations
- ○ Compassion – Tonglen
- ○ Lovingkindness - Maitri

How will I continue to care for myself today?_____
_____

My Journal for today... thoughts, notes, experiences...

Date: _____

Before you practice, check in with yourself.

- ❖ MIND

Quiet				Very Noisy
1	2	3	4	5

- ❖ BODY

Relaxed				Very Tense
1	2	3	4	5

- ❖ SPIRIT

At ease				Very Uneasy
1	2	3	4	5

The practice(s) I am working with today: (check which one(s) you feel drawn to)

- ○ Body scan
- ○ Release Your Tension
- ○ Calm-abiding Meditation
- ○ Contemplations
- ○ Compassion – Tonglen
- ○ Lovingkindness - Maitri

How will I continue to care for myself today?_____
_____

My Journal for today… thoughts, notes, experiences…

Date: _____

Before you practice, check in with yourself.

- ❖ MIND

    Quiet   Very Noisy

    1   2   3   4   5

- ❖ BODY

    Relaxed   Very Tense

    1   2   3   4   5

- ❖ SPIRIT

    At ease   Very Uneasy

    1   2   3   4   5

The practice(s) I am working with today: (check which one(s) you feel drawn to)

- ○ Body scan
- ○ Release Your Tension
- ○ Calm-abiding Meditation
- ○ Contemplations
- ○ Compassion – Tonglen
- ○ Lovingkindness - Maitri

How will I continue to care for myself today?_____

_____

My Journal for today... thoughts, notes, experiences...

Date: _____

Before you practice, check in with yourself.

- ❖ MIND

  Quiet   Very Noisy

  1   2   3   4   5

- ❖ BODY

  Relaxed   Very Tense

  1   2   3   4   5

- ❖ SPIRIT

  At ease   Very Uneasy

  1   2   3   4   5

The practice(s) I am working with today: (check which one(s) you feel drawn to)

- ○ Body scan
- ○ Release Your Tension
- ○ Calm-abiding Meditation
- ○ Contemplations
- ○ Compassion – Tonglen
- ○ Lovingkindness - Maitri

How will I continue to care for myself today?_____

_____

My Journal for today… thoughts, notes, experiences…

Date: _____

Before you practice, check in with yourself.

- ❖ MIND

Quiet				Very Noisy
1	2	3	4	5

- ❖ BODY

Relaxed				Very Tense
1	2	3	4	5

- ❖ SPIRIT

At ease				Very Uneasy
1	2	3	4	5

The practice(s) I am working with today: (check which one(s) you feel drawn to)

- ○ Body scan
- ○ Release Your Tension
- ○ Calm-abiding Meditation
- ○ Contemplations
- ○ Compassion – Tonglen
- ○ Lovingkindness - Maitri

How will I continue to care for myself today?_____

_____

My Journal for today… thoughts, notes, experiences…

Date: _____

Before you practice, check in with yourself.

- ❖ MIND

Quiet				Very Noisy
1	2	3	4	5

- ❖ BODY

Relaxed				Very Tense
1	2	3	4	5

- ❖ SPIRIT

At ease				Very Uneasy
1	2	3	4	5

The practice(s) I am working with today: (check which one(s) you feel drawn to)

- ○ Body scan
- ○ Release Your Tension
- ○ Calm-abiding Meditation
- ○ Contemplations
- ○ Compassion – Tonglen
- ○ Lovingkindness - Maitri

How will I continue to care for myself today?_____
_____

My Journal for today… thoughts, notes, experiences…

Date: _____

Before you practice, check in with yourself.

- ❖ MIND

Quiet				Very Noisy
1	2	3	4	5

- ❖ BODY

Relaxed				Very Tense
1	2	3	4	5

- ❖ SPIRIT

At ease				Very Uneasy
1	2	3	4	5

The practice(s) I am working with today: (check which one(s) you feel drawn to)

- ○ Body scan
- ○ Release Your Tension
- ○ Calm-abiding Meditation
- ○ Contemplations
- ○ Compassion – Tonglen
- ○ Lovingkindness - Maitri

How will I continue to care for myself today?_____

_____

My Journal for today… thoughts, notes, experiences…

Date: _____

Before you practice, check in with yourself.

- ❖ MIND

    Quiet   Very Noisy

    1   2   3   4   5

- ❖ BODY

    Relaxed   Very Tense

    1   2   3   4   5

- ❖ SPIRIT

    At ease   Very Uneasy

    1   2   3   4   5

The practice(s) I am working with today: (check which one(s) you feel drawn to)

- ❍ Body scan
- ❍ Release Your Tension
- ❍ Calm-abiding Meditation
- ❍ Contemplations
- ❍ Compassion – Tonglen
- ❍ Lovingkindness - Maitri

How will I continue to care for myself today?_____

_____

My Journal for today… thoughts, notes, experiences…

Date: _____

Before you practice, check in with yourself.

- ❖ MIND

Quiet				Very Noisy
1	2	3	4	5

- ❖ BODY

Relaxed				Very Tense
1	2	3	4	5

- ❖ SPIRIT

At ease				Very Uneasy
1	2	3	4	5

The practice(s) I am working with today: (check which one(s) you feel drawn to)

- ○ Body scan
- ○ Release Your Tension
- ○ Calm-abiding Meditation
- ○ Contemplations
- ○ Compassion – Tonglen
- ○ Lovingkindness - Maitri

How will I continue to care for myself today?_____
_____

My Journal for today… thoughts, notes, experiences…

Date: _____

Before you practice, check in with yourself.

- ❖ MIND

Quiet				Very Noisy
1	2	3	4	5

- ❖ BODY

Relaxed				Very Tense
1	2	3	4	5

- ❖ SPIRIT

At ease				Very Uneasy
1	2	3	4	5

The practice(s) I am working with today: (check which one(s) you feel drawn to)
- ○ Body scan
- ○ Release Your Tension
- ○ Calm-abiding Meditation
- ○ Contemplations
- ○ Compassion – Tonglen
- ○ Lovingkindness - Maitri

How will I continue to care for myself today?_____
_____

My Journal for today… thoughts, notes, experiences…

Date: _____

Before you practice, check in with yourself.

- ❖ MIND

Quiet				Very Noisy
1	2	3	4	5

- ❖ BODY

Relaxed				Very Tense
1	2	3	4	5

- ❖ SPIRIT

At ease				Very Uneasy
1	2	3	4	5

The practice(s) I am working with today: (check which one(s) you feel drawn to)
- ○ Body scan
- ○ Release Your Tension
- ○ Calm-abiding Meditation
- ○ Contemplations
- ○ Compassion – Tonglen
- ○ Lovingkindness - Maitri

How will I continue to care for myself today?_____
_____

My Journal for today... thoughts, notes, experiences...

Date: _____

Before you practice, check in with yourself.

- ❖ MIND

  Quiet   Very Noisy

  1   2   3   4   5

- ❖ BODY

  Relaxed   Very Tense

  1   2   3   4   5

- ❖ SPIRIT

  At ease   Very Uneasy

  1   2   3   4   5

The practice(s) I am working with today: (check which one(s) you feel drawn to)

- ○ Body scan
- ○ Release Your Tension
- ○ Calm-abiding Meditation
- ○ Contemplations
- ○ Compassion – Tonglen
- ○ Lovingkindness - Maitri

How will I continue to care for myself today?_____

_____

My Journal for today... thoughts, notes, experiences...

Date: _____

Before you practice, check in with yourself.

- ❖ MIND

Quiet				Very Noisy
1	2	3	4	5

- ❖ BODY

Relaxed				Very Tense
1	2	3	4	5

- ❖ SPIRIT

At ease				Very Uneasy
1	2	3	4	5

The practice(s) I am working with today: (check which one(s) you feel drawn to)

- ○ Body scan
- ○ Release Your Tension
- ○ Calm-abiding Meditation
- ○ Contemplations
- ○ Compassion – Tonglen
- ○ Lovingkindness - Maitri

How will I continue to care for myself today?_____

_____

My Journal for today... thoughts, notes, experiences...

Date: _____

Before you practice, check in with yourself.

- ❖ MIND

Quiet				Very Noisy
1	2	3	4	5

- ❖ BODY

Relaxed				Very Tense
1	2	3	4	5

- ❖ SPIRIT

At ease				Very Uneasy
1	2	3	4	5

The practice(s) I am working with today: (check which one(s) you feel drawn to)

- ❍ Body scan
- ❍ Release Your Tension
- ❍ Calm-abiding Meditation
- ❍ Contemplations
- ❍ Compassion – Tonglen
- ❍ Lovingkindness - Maitri

How will I continue to care for myself today?_____

_____

My Journal for today... thoughts, notes, experiences...

Date: _____

Before you practice, check in with yourself.

- ❖ MIND

  Quiet   Very Noisy

  1   2   3   4   5

- ❖ BODY

  Relaxed   Very Tense

  1   2   3   4   5

- ❖ SPIRIT

  At ease   Very Uneasy

  1   2   3   4   5

The practice(s) I am working with today: (check which one(s) you feel drawn to)

- ○ Body scan
- ○ Release Your Tension
- ○ Calm-abiding Meditation
- ○ Contemplations
- ○ Compassion – Tonglen
- ○ Lovingkindness - Maitri

How will I continue to care for myself today?_____

_____

My Journal for today… thoughts, notes, experiences…

Date: _____

Before you practice, check in with yourself.

- ❖ MIND

Quiet				Very Noisy
1	2	3	4	5

- ❖ BODY

Relaxed				Very Tense
1	2	3	4	5

- ❖ SPIRIT

At ease				Very Uneasy
1	2	3	4	5

The practice(s) I am working with today: (check which one(s) you feel drawn to)

- ○ Body scan
- ○ Release Your Tension
- ○ Calm-abiding Meditation
- ○ Contemplations
- ○ Compassion – Tonglen
- ○ Lovingkindness - Maitri

How will I continue to care for myself today?_____

_____

My Journal for today… thoughts, notes, experiences…

Date: _____

Before you practice, check in with yourself.

- ❖ MIND

Quiet				Very Noisy
1	2	3	4	5

- ❖ BODY

Relaxed				Very Tense
1	2	3	4	5

- ❖ SPIRIT

At ease				Very Uneasy
1	2	3	4	5

The practice(s) I am working with today: (check which one(s) you feel drawn to)

- ○ Body scan
- ○ Release Your Tension
- ○ Calm-abiding Meditation
- ○ Contemplations
- ○ Compassion – Tonglen
- ○ Lovingkindness - Maitri

How will I continue to care for myself today?_____

_____

My Journal for today… thoughts, notes, experiences…

Date: _____

Before you practice, check in with yourself.

- ❖ MIND

Quiet				Very Noisy
1	2	3	4	5

- ❖ BODY

Relaxed				Very Tense
1	2	3	4	5

- ❖ SPIRIT

At ease				Very Uneasy
1	2	3	4	5

The practice(s) I am working with today: (check which one(s) you feel drawn to)

- ○ Body scan
- ○ Release Your Tension
- ○ Calm-abiding Meditation
- ○ Contemplations
- ○ Compassion – Tonglen
- ○ Lovingkindness - Maitri

How will I continue to care for myself today?_____

_____

My Journal for today... thoughts, notes, experiences...

Date: _____

Before you practice, check in with yourself.

- ❖ MIND

Quiet				Very Noisy
1	2	3	4	5

- ❖ BODY

Relaxed				Very Tense
1	2	3	4	5

- ❖ SPIRIT

At ease				Very Uneasy
1	2	3	4	5

The practice(s) I am working with today: (check which one(s) you feel drawn to)
- ○ Body scan
- ○ Release Your Tension
- ○ Calm-abiding Meditation
- ○ Contemplations
- ○ Compassion – Tonglen
- ○ Lovingkindness - Maitri

How will I continue to care for myself today?_____
_____

My Journal for today... thoughts, notes, experiences...

Date: _____

Before you practice, check in with yourself.

- ❖ MIND

Quiet				Very Noisy
1	2	3	4	5

- ❖ BODY

Relaxed				Very Tense
1	2	3	4	5

- ❖ SPIRIT

At ease				Very Uneasy
1	2	3	4	5

The practice(s) I am working with today: (check which one(s) you feel drawn to)

- ○ Body scan
- ○ Release Your Tension
- ○ Calm-abiding Meditation
- ○ Contemplations
- ○ Compassion – Tonglen
- ○ Lovingkindness - Maitri

How will I continue to care for myself today?_____
_____

My Journal for today... thoughts, notes, experiences...

Date: _____

Before you practice, check in with yourself.

- ❖ MIND

Quiet				Very Noisy
1	2	3	4	5

- ❖ BODY

Relaxed				Very Tense
1	2	3	4	5

- ❖ SPIRIT

At ease				Very Uneasy
1	2	3	4	5

The practice(s) I am working with today: (check which one(s) you feel drawn to)

- ○ Body scan
- ○ Release Your Tension
- ○ Calm-abiding Meditation
- ○ Contemplations
- ○ Compassion – Tonglen
- ○ Lovingkindness - Maitri

How will I continue to care for myself today?_____
_____

My Journal for today… thoughts, notes, experiences…

Date: _____

Before you practice, check in with yourself.

- ❖ MIND

Quiet				Very Noisy
1	2	3	4	5

- ❖ BODY

Relaxed				Very Tense
1	2	3	4	5

- ❖ SPIRIT

At ease				Very Uneasy
1	2	3	4	5

The practice(s) I am working with today: (check which one(s) you feel drawn to)

- ○ Body scan
- ○ Release Your Tension
- ○ Calm-abiding Meditation
- ○ Contemplations
- ○ Compassion – Tonglen
- ○ Lovingkindness - Maitri

How will I continue to care for myself today?_____

_____

My Journal for today... thoughts, notes, experiences...

Date: _____

Before you practice, check in with yourself.

- ❖ MIND

Quiet				Very Noisy
1	2	3	4	5

- ❖ BODY

Relaxed				Very Tense
1	2	3	4	5

- ❖ SPIRIT

At ease				Very Uneasy
1	2	3	4	5

The practice(s) I am working with today: (check which one(s) you feel drawn to)

- ○ Body scan
- ○ Release Your Tension
- ○ Calm-abiding Meditation
- ○ Contemplations
- ○ Compassion – Tonglen
- ○ Lovingkindness - Maitri

How will I continue to care for myself today?_____

_____

My Journal for today… thoughts, notes, experiences…

Date: _____

Before you practice, check in with yourself.

- ❖ MIND

  Quiet   Very Noisy

  1   2   3   4   5

- ❖ BODY

  Relaxed   Very Tense

  1   2   3   4   5

- ❖ SPIRIT

  At ease   Very Uneasy

  1   2   3   4   5

The practice(s) I am working with today: (check which one(s) you feel drawn to)

- ○ Body scan
- ○ Release Your Tension
- ○ Calm-abiding Meditation
- ○ Contemplations
- ○ Compassion – Tonglen
- ○ Lovingkindness - Maitri

How will I continue to care for myself today?_____

_____

My Journal for today… thoughts, notes, experiences…

Date: _____

Before you practice, check in with yourself.

- ❖ MIND

Quiet				Very Noisy
1	2	3	4	5

- ❖ BODY

Relaxed				Very Tense
1	2	3	4	5

- ❖ SPIRIT

At ease				Very Uneasy
1	2	3	4	5

The practice(s) I am working with today: (check which one(s) you feel drawn to)

- ○ Body scan
- ○ Release Your Tension
- ○ Calm-abiding Meditation
- ○ Contemplations
- ○ Compassion – Tonglen
- ○ Lovingkindness - Maitri

How will I continue to care for myself today? _____

_____

My Journal for today… thoughts, notes, experiences…

Date: _____

Before you practice, check in with yourself.

- ❖ MIND

Quiet				Very Noisy
1	2	3	4	5

- ❖ BODY

Relaxed				Very Tense
1	2	3	4	5

- ❖ SPIRIT

At ease				Very Uneasy
1	2	3	4	5

The practice(s) I am working with today: (check which one(s) you feel drawn to)

- ○ Body scan
- ○ Release Your Tension
- ○ Calm-abiding Meditation
- ○ Contemplations
- ○ Compassion – Tonglen
- ○ Lovingkindness - Maitri

How will I continue to care for myself today?_____

_____

My Journal for today… thoughts, notes, experiences…

Date: _____

Before you practice, check in with yourself.

- ❖ MIND

Quiet				Very Noisy
1	2	3	4	5

- ❖ BODY

Relaxed				Very Tense
1	2	3	4	5

- ❖ SPIRIT

At ease				Very Uneasy
1	2	3	4	5

The practice(s) I am working with today: (check which one(s) you feel drawn to)

- ○ Body scan
- ○ Release Your Tension
- ○ Calm-abiding Meditation
- ○ Contemplations
- ○ Compassion – Tonglen
- ○ Lovingkindness - Maitri

How will I continue to care for myself today?_____

_____

My Journal for today… thoughts, notes, experiences…

Date: _____

Before you practice, check in with yourself.

- ❖ MIND

Quiet				Very Noisy
1	2	3	4	5

- ❖ BODY

Relaxed				Very Tense
1	2	3	4	5

- ❖ SPIRIT

At ease				Very Uneasy
1	2	3	4	5

The practice(s) I am working with today: (check which one(s) you feel drawn to)
- ○ Body scan
- ○ Release Your Tension
- ○ Calm-abiding Meditation
- ○ Contemplations
- ○ Compassion – Tonglen
- ○ Lovingkindness - Maitri

How will I continue to care for myself today?_____
_____

My Journal for today… thoughts, notes, experiences…

Date: _____

Before you practice, check in with yourself.

- ❖ MIND

  Quiet   Very Noisy

  1   2   3   4   5

- ❖ BODY

  Relaxed   Very Tense

  1   2   3   4   5

- ❖ SPIRIT

  At ease   Very Uneasy

  1   2   3   4   5

The practice(s) I am working with today: (check which one(s) you feel drawn to)
- ○ Body scan
- ○ Release Your Tension
- ○ Calm-abiding Meditation
- ○ Contemplations
- ○ Compassion – Tonglen
- ○ Lovingkindness - Maitri

How will I continue to care for myself today?_____

_____

My Journal for today… thoughts, notes, experiences…

Date: _____

Before you practice, check in with yourself.

- ❖ MIND

  Quiet   Very Noisy

  1   2   3   4   5

- ❖ BODY

  Relaxed   Very Tense

  1   2   3   4   5

- ❖ SPIRIT

  At ease   Very Uneasy

  1   2   3   4   5

The practice(s) I am working with today: (check which one(s) you feel drawn to)
- ○ Body scan
- ○ Release Your Tension
- ○ Calm-abiding Meditation
- ○ Contemplations
- ○ Compassion – Tonglen
- ○ Lovingkindness - Maitri

How will I continue to care for myself today?_____

_____

My Journal for today... thoughts, notes, experiences...

ef

Date: _____

Before you practice, check in with yourself.

- ❖ MIND

Quiet				Very Noisy
1	2	3	4	5

- ❖ BODY

Relaxed				Very Tense
1	2	3	4	5

- ❖ SPIRIT

At ease				Very Uneasy
1	2	3	4	5

The practice(s) I am working with today: (check which one(s) you feel drawn to)
- ○ Body scan
- ○ Release Your Tension
- ○ Calm-abiding Meditation
- ○ Contemplations
- ○ Compassion – Tonglen
- ○ Lovingkindness - Maitri

How will I continue to care for myself today?_____
_____

My Journal for today… thoughts, notes, experiences…

Date: _____

Before you practice, check in with yourself.

- ❖ MIND

Quiet				Very Noisy
1	2	3	4	5

- ❖ BODY

Relaxed				Very Tense
1	2	3	4	5

- ❖ SPIRIT

At ease				Very Uneasy
1	2	3	4	5

The practice(s) I am working with today: (check which one(s) you feel drawn to)
- ○ Body scan
- ○ Release Your Tension
- ○ Calm-abiding Meditation
- ○ Contemplations
- ○ Compassion – Tonglen
- ○ Lovingkindness - Maitri

How will I continue to care for myself today?_____
_____

My Journal for today… thoughts, notes, experiences…

Date: _____

Before you practice, check in with yourself.

- ❖ MIND

    Quiet   Very Noisy

    1   2   3   4   5

- ❖ BODY

    Relaxed   Very Tense

    1   2   3   4   5

- ❖ SPIRIT

    At ease   Very Uneasy

    1   2   3   4   5

The practice(s) I am working with today: (check which one(s) you feel drawn to)
- ○ Body scan
- ○ Release Your Tension
- ○ Calm-abiding Meditation
- ○ Contemplations
- ○ Compassion – Tonglen
- ○ Lovingkindness - Maitri

How will I continue to care for myself today?_____

_____

My Journal for today… thoughts, notes, experiences…

Date: _____

Before you practice, check in with yourself.

- ❖ MIND

Quiet				Very Noisy
1	2	3	4	5

- ❖ BODY

Relaxed				Very Tense
1	2	3	4	5

- ❖ SPIRIT

At ease				Very Uneasy
1	2	3	4	5

The practice(s) I am working with today: (check which one(s) you feel drawn to)

- ○ Body scan
- ○ Release Your Tension
- ○ Calm-abiding Meditation
- ○ Contemplations
- ○ Compassion – Tonglen
- ○ Lovingkindness - Maitri

How will I continue to care for myself today?_____
_____

My Journal for today... thoughts, notes, experiences...

Date: _____

Before you practice, check in with yourself.

- ❖ MIND

Quiet				Very Noisy
1	2	3	4	5

- ❖ BODY

Relaxed				Very Tense
1	2	3	4	5

- ❖ SPIRIT

At ease				Very Uneasy
1	2	3	4	5

The practice(s) I am working with today: (check which one(s) you feel drawn to)

- ○ Body scan
- ○ Release Your Tension
- ○ Calm-abiding Meditation
- ○ Contemplations
- ○ Compassion – Tonglen
- ○ Lovingkindness - Maitri

How will I continue to care for myself today?_____

_____

My Journal for today… thoughts, notes, experiences…

Date: _____

Before you practice, check in with yourself.

- ❖ MIND

  QuietVery Noisy

  12345

- ❖ BODY

  RelaxedVery Tense

  12345

- ❖ SPIRIT

  At easeVery Uneasy

  12345

The practice(s) I am working with today: (check which one(s) you feel drawn to)

- ○ Body scan
- ○ Release Your Tension
- ○ Calm-abiding Meditation
- ○ Contemplations
- ○ Compassion – Tonglen
- ○ Lovingkindness - Maitri

How will I continue to care for myself today?_____

_____

My Journal for today… thoughts, notes, experiences…

Date: _____

Before you practice, check in with yourself.

- ❖ MIND

Quiet				Very Noisy
1	2	3	4	5

- ❖ BODY

Relaxed				Very Tense
1	2	3	4	5

- ❖ SPIRIT

At ease				Very Uneasy
1	2	3	4	5

The practice(s) I am working with today: (check which one(s) you feel drawn to)

- ○ Body scan
- ○ Release Your Tension
- ○ Calm-abiding Meditation
- ○ Contemplations
- ○ Compassion – Tonglen
- ○ Lovingkindness - Maitri

How will I continue to care for myself today?_____

_____

My Journal for today… thoughts, notes, experiences…

Date: _____

Before you practice, check in with yourself.

- ❖ MIND

Quiet				Very Noisy
1	2	3	4	5

- ❖ BODY

Relaxed				Very Tense
1	2	3	4	5

- ❖ SPIRIT

At ease				Very Uneasy
1	2	3	4	5

The practice(s) I am working with today: (check which one(s) you feel drawn to)
- ○ Body scan
- ○ Release Your Tension
- ○ Calm-abiding Meditation
- ○ Contemplations
- ○ Compassion – Tonglen
- ○ Lovingkindness - Maitri

How will I continue to care for myself today?_____

_____

My Journal for today… thoughts, notes, experiences…

Date: _____

Before you practice, check in with yourself.

- ❖ MIND

Quiet				Very Noisy
1	2	3	4	5

- ❖ BODY

Relaxed				Very Tense
1	2	3	4	5

- ❖ SPIRIT

At ease				Very Uneasy
1	2	3	4	5

The practice(s) I am working with today: (check which one(s) you feel drawn to)
- ○ Body scan
- ○ Release Your Tension
- ○ Calm-abiding Meditation
- ○ Contemplations
- ○ Compassion – Tonglen
- ○ Lovingkindness - Maitri

How will I continue to care for myself today?_____

_____

My Journal for today… thoughts, notes, experiences…

Date: _____

Before you practice, check in with yourself.

- ❖ MIND

Quiet				Very Noisy
1	2	3	4	5

- ❖ BODY

Relaxed				Very Tense
1	2	3	4	5

- ❖ SPIRIT

At ease				Very Uneasy
1	2	3	4	5

The practice(s) I am working with today: (check which one(s) you feel drawn to)

- ○ Body scan
- ○ Release Your Tension
- ○ Calm-abiding Meditation
- ○ Contemplations
- ○ Compassion – Tonglen
- ○ Lovingkindness - Maitri

How will I continue to care for myself today?_____

_____

My Journal for today… thoughts, notes, experiences…

Date: _____

Before you practice, check in with yourself.

- ❖ MIND

    Quiet   Very Noisy

    1   2   3   4   5

- ❖ BODY

    Relaxed   Very Tense

    1   2   3   4   5

- ❖ SPIRIT

    At ease   Very Uneasy

    1   2   3   4   5

The practice(s) I am working with today: (check which one(s) you feel drawn to)
- ○ Body scan
- ○ Release Your Tension
- ○ Calm-abiding Meditation
- ○ Contemplations
- ○ Compassion – Tonglen
- ○ Lovingkindness - Maitri

How will I continue to care for myself today?_____

_____

My Journal for today… thoughts, notes, experiences…

Date: _____

Before you practice, check in with yourself.

- ❖ MIND

Quiet				Very Noisy
1	2	3	4	5

- ❖ BODY

Relaxed				Very Tense
1	2	3	4	5

- ❖ SPIRIT

At ease				Very Uneasy
1	2	3	4	5

The practice(s) I am working with today: (check which one(s) you feel drawn to)
- ○ Body scan
- ○ Release Your Tension
- ○ Calm-abiding Meditation
- ○ Contemplations
- ○ Compassion – Tonglen
- ○ Lovingkindness - Maitri

How will I continue to care for myself today?_____
_____

My Journal for today… thoughts, notes, experiences…

Appendix: Practices

Excerpts from Unwinding Anxiety: Free Your Mind, Get Your Life Back

Excerpt from: Mindfulness and Awareness Starts With the Body

Practice: Simply noticing without judging.

Part of anxiety is that we don't feel safe. Fears arise then flush through the psyche and the body. For now, I would like you to trust that you're safe with yourself. There is no need to judge or criticize. As you work through this practice, you will notice your body in a very gentle way.

In this practice, you will gently bring your awareness to the body as we scan from bottom to top, and if something stands out, note it and let it go. Note the attributes like tight, loose, sore, pulsing, blocked, relaxed, neutral, or whatever you observe. Starting with the body is a good way to ground yourself. After your read the process, try it for yourself.

1. Close your eyes. Take a few slow, deep breaths.

2. Place awareness in the body. Scan the body one spot at a time, starting with the soles of your feet. You can follow the steps that follow this. I would also suggest that you bring awareness to one spot at a time if there is a right and a left. Do the right foot, then the left foot, right cheek, then left cheek.

3. One thing that is helpful is to scan the body, with only a brief stay at each spot. Keep your awareness moving, until you're the whole way through the scan.

4. If thoughts come up, let them go and follow your mind to the next spot on your body.

5. As you scan, notice tension or looseness, but don't add commentary to it. If a storyline pops up about why something hurts and feels good,

drop it and return to the scan of the body. Take a deep breath, then release.

6. Here is the suggested pattern, though it is up to you. Don't make it about rules. Just play with it and be comfortable.

    Feet: *Soles, toes, tops of feet, ankles*

    Legs: *Shins, calves, knees front and back, thighs, hamstrings*

    Pelvic area: *hip sides, buttocks, groin*

    Abdomen: *Lower belly, upper belly*

    Chest: *Start around the breastbone, then up to the collarbone, scanning the whole area*

    Torso: *Right side, Left side*

    Back: *Lower back, middle back, upper back*

    Hands: *Fingertips, knuckles, palms, back of hand*

    Arms: *Forearms, elbows, biceps, triceps*

    Shoulders: *Right side, left side*

    Neck and throat

Head: *all the way around from back to front and bottom to top, ears, forehead, nose, lips, cheeks, chin, mouth*

7. How did it feel? When is the last time you connected to your body like this, simply noticing without commentary and critique?

8. One thing that is helpful is to scan the body, with only a brief stay at each spot. Keep your awareness moving, until you're the whole way through the scan.

9. If thoughts come up, let them go and follow your mind to the next spot on your body.

10. Repeat this exercise at least once a day, but preferably twice, to remind yourself to check in with your body. Do it every day for 7 days, noting patterns.

Practice: Tighten and Release

1. Scan your body using the pattern listed below. As you come to each body part, tighten or clench them while inhaling

2. Relax the body part and exhale. Move to the next spot.

    Tighten and Release Pattern:

    Whole Body... then

    Feet: *Soles, toes, tops of feet, ankles*

    Legs: *Shins, calves, knees front and back, thighs, hamstrings,*

    Pelvic area: *hip sides, buttocks, groin,*

    Abdomen: *Lower belly, upper belly*

    Chest and Back: *as a whole*

    Hands: *Fingertips, knuckles, palms, back of hand*

    Arms and shoulders: *Forearms, elbows, biceps, triceps*

    Head: *eyes, forehead, mouth, face.*

    Finally, feel the body as a whole.

Excerpt from: What is Meditation and Why Bother?

Some things to know about meditation:

1. It isn't about stopping your mind. Instead you work with whatever arises.

2. You don't have to burn incense or candles, unless it makes you happy.

3. You don't need special cushions, unless it is something you want. You can do it in a chair if that works better for you. A chair, a pillow, a yoga mat, the floor – all of these are fine.

4. You can do it in small increments, from seconds or minutes and work up over time.

5. It isn't a contest. There's no need to compare yourself to anyone else or their experience with these practices.

6. It isn't a contest. Be gentle with yourself because the process is simply an opportunity to know yourself better.

7. You don't have to believe in anything special. It's an exploration of the mind.

8. There are no special clothes. Just wear something comfortable and stretchy.

9. There is no right or wrong, good or bad meditation.

10. You can wiggle. It's okay.

Excerpt from: Meditation – How it Works

You may be wondering about what the room should be like. Lights? Music? Candles? Incense?

Light a candle or incense if you enjoy it, but no "smells and bells" are required. Use them if it pleases you. However, regarding music, it is best to have a quiet space for the kind of meditation I am explaining.

Shamatha – or Calm-Abiding -Meditation.

Physical posture...

- **So, start by taking your seat.**

If you're on a pillow or cushion, gently cross your legs. Don't worry about things like full and half lotus positions. Simply cross your legs in a comfortable position.

- **If you're in a chair, plant your feet on the floor**.

If the chair is too tall for you, grab a pillow to rest your feet on. Sit slightly forward in the chair, not resting against the back of the seat unless you have a physical condition that requires the extra support. It is helpful to scoot forward in the seat a little so it isn't so easy to lean back.

- **In order to find a stable and comfortable position, begin by rocking back and forth, side to side gently**. Your "sit bones" are the bones in your buttocks that give support when you sit upright.

- **Place your hands on your lap,**

- **Get a sense of the position of your head, neck, and chin**.

They should be aligned nicely, not too far forward or backward, which causes strain in the muscles.

- **Notice how your body feels.**

Generally, this should be a comfortable, stable, upright, and uplifted position that you can hold for the time you're meditating. Make slight adjustments, gently modifying your position as needed.

- **One question is if your eyes should be open or closed.**

For the purposes of this meditation style, we do it with open eyes. Let your gaze settle about four to six feet in front of you. There is no need to stare hard at the floor. **Keep a soft gaze, not focused on any one spot**.

Mind and Breath Together

For a moment you might try closing your eyes and taking a few slow, deep breaths. This will help center you. When you're ready, open your eyes.

Mindfulness is following the breath – placing the mind on the inhalations, exhalations, and the space between them. Awareness is noticing you're no longer with the breath.

Breathing

- **As you sit, place your attention on the breath going in and out of your body.** Breathe normally. There's no need to take deep breaths or shallow breaths. Instead breathe like you always do. In then out. Nice and steady.

- **Continue with your awareness on the breath.** As it leaves your body, let whatever is happening in you dissolve on the outbreath.
- **Experience the slight gap or pause between breaths.**

Thinking and Returning

When your mind wanders off, you may not notice for a little while, seconds or minutes. **Don't worry, but when you do notice, just return your focus to the breathing body.** Feel how the breath flows in and out of you, expanding, contracting, the rise and fall of your abdomen and chest.

You may want to label the thought as "thinking." There are a variety of methods for this. But as you begin this practice, this method is quite simple and helpful. The key is to not judge the thought or yourself for having the thought.

Meditation isn't about the quality of the thoughts. It is about returning to the breath over and over. No thought is more important than another, no better, no worse. Stabilizing your mind comes from acknowledging

<u>the thought, dropping it, and shifting focus back to how the breath enters and exits the body.</u>

Those are the bare bones of meditation practice. Now, let me share other things to notice or consider when doing it.

How does meditation help dismantle anxiety?

Even though I'd been doing meditation for a few years, <u>I hadn't tried applying it in the midst of an anxiety or panic attack.</u> And then I did. And it started to work, bit by bit.

Let me just suggest it is good if you experiment with meditation when things are a little more calm for you. But if you're really suffering right now, don't wait for it to pass. Even deep in anxiety, it is workable.

You may be experiencing fierce anxiousness. Let me encourage you to start now, wherever and however you feel. **The simplest relief will come from breathing. The long lasting relief comes from the practice of letting go of whatever is on your mind as you return to the breath. It sounds simplistic**.

Not much different from curling a dumbbell to grow stronger biceps. Or doing yoga to get stability in your core. This is a process and an exercise that strengthens and gives flexibility to your mind and heart.

Excerpt from: Slow Down, You Move Too Fast

Practice: Slow Walking

Stand in place for a moment or two and concentrate on the feeling of the ground beneath you. What does it feel like to stand there?

Let your arms rest comfortably by your side.

Begin walking at about half the speed you normally do. There are reasons for this. First, this isn't an aerobic workout for your body, though the body will certainly reap benefit from it. Second, it is hard to keep the mind focused when you're going faster.

Give yourself permission to slow down. As you move forward, let your mind come to rest on the sensation of each foot connecting with the ground.

Feel the heels and balls of your feet, the flex of the arch, the rolling of the foot as it takes each step.

When the mind starts to worry or daydream or make to-do lists or fantasize, bring the attention back to the feet.

Once you've connected your focus with your feet and their motion, expand your awareness. Be mindful of the environment you're in, but don't comment or label. Just experience the conditions as you step, step, step. It's a light touch, this focus we bring to the practice of slow walking.

Notice the wind against your skin. Is the sun shining? What does the temperature feel like? Feel snowflakes. Walk around the puddle or through it. While walking through the grass, notice the hole you need to avoid. What surface are you walking on? Notice the differences and what comes up for you.

The nice thing about this practice is you can do it anywhere you can walk. Relax the pressure. Nowhere to get to, just a slow easy jaunt in the freshness of nature. How does it feel?

Play around with your gaze. Where do your eyes land?

What is it like to focus in front of you at the ground?

What about if you raise your eyes and look straight out, noticing what is in front of you ten or twenty feet ahead?

Is it easier to focus on the feet if you're looking from side to side, a panoramic view?

What does it feel like to not comment on everything, only walk through and notice it?

It is helpful to be experience these suggestions and find what gives you the most relief. By focusing the mind, you will start to have awareness of even the slightest changes in your emotions and mindset as well as how your body feels.

How long and how often?

Start small. Just five minutes. Build up. Don't be afraid to go for longer, working up to twenty or thirty minutes.

Excerpt from: Contemplations

Many years ago, I read this story and it stayed with me all this time. Something about the possibilities of looking at life differently and with more ease keep drawing me back to it. I share it often with people I sense are in distress or troubled times. Perhaps you've encountered this story also, but it is worth revisiting.

The Parable of the Chinese Farmer

Once there was a Chinese farmer who worked his poor farm together with his son and their horse. When the horse ran off one day, neighbors came to say, "How unfortunate for you!" The farmer replied, "Maybe yes, maybe no."

When the horse returned, followed by a herd of wild horses, the neighbors gathered around and exclaimed, "What good luck for you!" The farmer stayed calm and replied, "Maybe yes, maybe no."

While trying to tame one of wild horses, the farmer's son fell, and broke his leg. He had to rest up and couldn't help with the farm chores. "How sad for you," the neighbors cried. "Maybe yes, maybe no," said the farmer.

Shortly thereafter, a neighboring army threatened the farmer's village. All the young men in the village were drafted to fight the invaders. Many died. But the farmer's son had been left out of the fighting because of his broken leg. People said to the farmer, "What a good thing your son couldn't fight!" "Maybe yes, maybe no," was all the farmer said.

###

Another story, I've read and want to share is this ancient story from the Sufi tradition. Once you've read it, do the same process in your journal, exploring what arises as you read it. Again, I ask you, how does it feel? Why do you think you feel this way?

This Too Shall Pass

According to an ancient Sufi story, there lived a king in some Middle Eastern land who was continuously torn between happiness and despondency. The slightest thing would cause him great upset or provoke an intense reaction and his happiness would quickly turn into disappointment and despair. A time came when the king finally got tired of himself and of his life so he began to seek a way out. He sent for a wise man who lived in the kingdom who was reputed and enlightened. When the wise man arrived, the king said to him, "I want to be like you. Can you give me something that will bring balance, serenity and wisdom into my life? I will pay any price you ask.

The wise man said, "I may be able to help you but the price is so great that your entire kingdom would not be sufficient payment for it. Therefore it will be a gift to you if you will honor it." The king gave his assurances and the wise man left. A few weeks later, he returned and handed the king an ornate box carved in jade. The king opened the box and found a simple gold ring inside. Some letters were inscribed on the ring. The inscription read: This, too, shall pass. "What is the meaning of this?" asked the king. The wise man replied, "Wear this ring always. Whatever happens, before you call it good or bad, touch this ring and read the inscription. That way, you will always be at peace."

Excerpt from: Compassion

One of the gentlest but bravest ways to find freedom over anxiety or any difficult emotion is to look at it and sit with it. By doing this, we start to see the emotion for what it is and where it comes from. Then we can extend kindness to it and ourselves.

Anxiety often feels like war or like we are being betrayed by our bodies and minds. Working with intentions and attention is a powerful way of making peace with yourself and others. The exercises that follow are well worth the effort.

Intention. What is it? A bit like a wish or a hope, but it needs a little more effort. It's like a focused, energetic wish or hope where you put some mojo into it, some juice, some jazz, some thunder. The wish or hope is filled with vitality through expression and heart.

I'd like to share with you a practice known as tonglen. It involves taking in and sending out energy and imagery.

Practice: Tonglen... Take and Send (The aspect of sending myself relief was new to me.)

With intentions, it is important to stay loose. Shake your body gently. Dangle and wiggle your arms around. Rock in your seat till you're comfortable. Rotate your neck gently. Try smiling, whether you feel like it or not. Then breathe in.

Get comfortable. You can sit or lie down, it doesn't matter. Start by centering yourself with a few breaths. First the breaths will slow you down, give you some space to do the next things.

Tonglen involves taking in the suffering of someone and sending out what you wish them to have. As an example, if you see someone fighting an illness, you can visualize taking in their suffering and sending out to them healthiness. Or it could be as simple as noticing someone is really tired and sending them alertness. Or a mental cup of coffee.

I find this works best with eyes closed, but do it either way as long as you're able to visualize.

Bring to a mind a person. **You can start with yourself** or someone you care about, someone easy for you. Focus on what they are suffering. It could be anxiety or something else.

1. Deep breath in, then let it out.
2. Now, as you inhale again, feel the textures or see the colors of the emotional state. Get a sense of it, first with the quality. Is it sharp, dull, pointed, wooly, soft, damp, soggy, crispy?
3. Exhale.
4. **Take another breath and see the color of the emotion**. Work with it, taking more breaths and time as needed. On each exhale, watch it dissolve.

5. When you're ready, get close to the feeling. Bring it into your mind and heart as much as you're able. **Imagine what you want to give them to relieve their hurting.** Then visualize sending it

As an example, you know well the feelings of anxiety. You could hone in on one specific feeling or the experience of it in general. As you take it in for yourself or another person, imagine what you want to send them. Perhaps it is relief, freedom, liberation. Maybe it is a cooling sensation and a calm mind. Maybe it is a good night's sleep.

You might start doing tonglen for someone you care about, someone neutral, someone you have difficulty with, *and also for yourself*. Play with each of these. Oftentimes our anxiety stems from our relationships. Other times it arises from things within ourselves that we are contending with. **Most of it is our minds projecting into the future about unknown and uncertain outcomes.**

As you get to know your anxiety better through the process of working with your mind and body, you will have a better sense of what tonglen practice should involve for you. Trust yourself. Trust in the process. And if you don't trust it, explore that in your journal.

The aspect of sending myself relief was new to me. It is more than wishing. It is working with your energy and sending out new energy or energetic imaginations. I send myself and others looseness to replace the knot in the chest, or deep soothing breaths to replace the short, shallow and tight breaths. **What do you want to send to yourself?**

Excerpt from: Practicing Lovingkindness

Mindset is a really powerful tool, and if you don't work with it and take care of it, you will find your mind to be unhelpful. Our minds are our best friends and worst enemies. To be free from the hold of anxiety, it is important to cultivate a mindset of spaciousness and observation. This becomes possible through light touches, just gentle and incremental changes to how we handle what comes up. And into that mix, you can add a bit of love and appreciation for yourself.

There is a beautiful practice known as Maitri or Metta, both which mean Lovingkindness. It is a contemplation where you send out intention for yourself or others.

Let me offer you some words to work with. Try saying them aloud or to yourself, whatever feels comfortable.

Practice: Lovingkindness Contemplation

May all beings be free from suffering and the root of suffering.

May I be free from suffering and the root of suffering.

May all beings be free from anxiety and the root of anxiety.

May I be free from anxiety and the root of anxiety.

May all beings know happiness and the root of happiness.

May I know happiness and the root of happiness.

Repeat these slowly to yourself. If you're alone, try speaking them out loud. If you're in front of a mirror, say them to the reflection in the mirror. Explore what they mean to you, what they feel like in your mind and body.

How does this help you with anxiety? Anxiety stems from doubt, fear and apprehension. We lack trust in wisdom and happiness. Working purposefully to acknowledge that yes, we have suffering, anxiety, fear, but also happiness, peace, and joy available to us does something for us. Have you considered the root of any of these things? Play with it. See what happens.

It works on your insides, and chips away at anxiety and the hard crust that pretends it is there to protect you. Slowly or suddenly there is a waking up to the understanding that nothing is solid and forever, including the anxiety you experience.

It may sound scary at first, but there is tremendous liberation when for even a moment you know that this too shall pass, and that your anxiety is not a fixed state.

May you be well on your journey... continue to make friends with your mind.

Made in the USA
Monee, IL
14 March 2021